JourneyThrough™

Colossians & Philemon

30 Daily Insights from God's Word by **Mike Raiter**

Journey Through Colossians & Philemon
© 2015 by Michael David Raiter
All rights reserved.

Distributed by Discovery House®. Discovery House® is affiliated
with Our Daily Bread Ministries®.

Requests for permission to quote
from this book should be directed to:
Permissions Department
Discovery House
P.O. Box 3566
Grand Rapids, MI 49501
Or contact us by email at
permissionsdept@dhp.org

Design by Joshua Tan
Typeset by Mary Chang

ISBN 978-1-62707-937-2

Printed in the United States
First Printing in 2018

Foreword

"There will be more rejoicing in heaven over one sinner who repents than over ninety-nine righteous persons who do not need to repent" (Luke 15:7). How true, but that is not all. God cares about the initial act of repentance and faith and also our continued sanctification. He wants us to keep trusting and pleasing Him in all we do. The Lord wants runners who finish the race and finish strong.

However, there are many obstacles along the way in the Christian life: temptations, suffering, and persecution. There will also be those who would try to undermine our confidence in the gospel. But in Christ, His Word, and His church, we have all the resources we need to keep growing strong in Him.

And that is where reading Colossians and Philemon comes in. The apostle Paul uses these two short letters to encourage and challenge a young church of first-century believers to keep maturing as Christians. They have begun well, now they must finish just as strongly. That is also my prayer for you as we listen to the living words of God together.

To God be the glory,
Mike Raiter

We're glad you've decided to join us on a journey into a deeper relationship with Jesus Christ!

For over 60 years, we have been known for the devotional *Our Daily Bread*. Many readers enjoy the encouraging, inspiring, and relevant articles that point them to God and the wisdom and promises of His unchanging Word.

Building on the foundation of *Our Daily Bread*, we have developed this devotional series to help believers spend time with God in His Word, book by book. We trust this daily meditation on God's Word will draw you into a closer relationship with Him through our Lord and Savior, Jesus Christ.

How to use this resource

READ: This book is designed to be read alongside God's Word as you journey with Him. It offers explanatory notes to help you understand the Scriptures in fresh ways.

REFLECT: The questions are designed to help you respond to God and His Word, letting Him change you from the inside out.

RECORD: The space provided allows you to keep a diary of your journey as you record your thoughts and jot down your responses.

An Overview

Around AD 52, Paul preached daily in the city of Ephesus. From there the gospel spread across the whole region, including Colossae. About eight years later, Paul found himself under house arrest in Rome. Epaphras came to see him, bringing news of the church in Colossae. From his prison, Paul wrote to the church in Colossae—a church he probably hadn't actually visited, but with whom he felt a strong connection. He wrote to encourage them to be "rooted and built up in [Jesus]" (Colossians 2:7). Paul wanted the believers there to keep growing strong in Christ.

The Structure of Colossians

1:1–2:5	Paul's thanksgiving and prayer for the Colossians' maturity
2:6–23	Encouragement and warnings to keep growing in Christ
3:1–4:6	New life in Christ
4:7–18	Paul's greetings to his friends

And while in prison, Paul also wrote the epistle of Philemon. In it he tackled the problem of Onesimus, a runaway slave from Colossae. This tiny epistle gives us a wonderful example of how to exercise pastoral ministry in the church, showing how a person who is growing strong in Christ demonstrates true fellowship.

Key Verses

"So then, just as you received Christ Jesus as Lord, continue to live your lives in him, rooted and built up in him, strengthened in the faith as you were taught, and overflowing with thankfulness." —Colossians 2:6–7

Read Colossians 1:1–5

Welcome to Colossians, Paul's word of encouragement to the "holy and faithful" in Colossae. Having introduced himself, Paul immediately reminds the Colossians of how he prays for them. Paul's prayer is astonishing: "We always thank God" (v. 3). Imagine you were awoken in the middle of the night to the news that your house had just burned down, and then you decided to send an email to friends around the world seeking their prayers. How would you begin? I would say, "Pray for us," and then at length describe my awful situation. How stunning that Paul begins with thanksgiving. Why is that so remarkable? Paul is awaiting trial, probably under house arrest in Rome. But you would hardly know that from this letter. **Many of Paul's letters were written from prison, but most of them contain almost nothing about his own situation. They are full of thanksgiving and exhortations to those he writes to.**

And look at what Paul is thankful for. He has heard about their faith in Christ and their love for one another (v. 4). Why are the Colossians living such faithful, loving lives? Because of "the hope stored up for [them] in heaven" (v. 5). We too share in this hope—the new heaven and the new earth that we will soon occupy. It is because we know we will have such an incredible inheritance *then* that we are energized to keep on trusting God and loving one another *now*.

How did people who were faithless, loveless, and hopeless have their lives so amazingly turned around? How did this miracle take place in the Colossian believers' lives? It is only because of "the true message of the gospel" (v. 5). The gospel is, first and foremost, news. It is words that are spoken and heard. The fruits of faith and love spring to life when God's mighty Spirit takes His dynamic, truthful Word and plants it in the hearts of people. Paul has heard of this great work in the lives of these young believers and so, despite his terrible trial, he first gives thanks to God.

Why is being thankful so important for Christians? What spiritual blessings can you thank God for right now?

Think about the hope laid up for Christians in heaven. How could more reflection on this hope transform your daily living?

Day 2

Read Colossians 1:6–8

Paul is thankful to God that His powerful Word of Truth has borne the fruit of faith and love in the lives of the Christians in Colossae. And not just in their lives, but also "the gospel is bearing fruit and growing throughout the whole world" (v. 6). Do those words ring a bell? Where have you heard the words "be fruitful and increase" before? It was God's first command to humanity in Genesis 1:28. In the beginning, how did God bring men and women to life? We find the answer in Genesis 1:28, "God said to them" (NKJV). **And God's almighty Word, carrying His authority and power, made it possible for humans to reproduce and fill the earth. Today, God is re-creating men and women in the image of His Son by the same powerful Word.**

So, how do we grow the church? Yes, we should research, plan, and strategize. But, fundamentally, faith, love, and hope spring to life in people's hearts by God's Word of Truth. Therefore, like Paul and Epaphras (Colossians 1:7), we must speak this gospel.

This gospel begins to bear fruit in people's lives once they have "heard it and truly understood God's grace" (v. 6). But, of course, you can listen to the gospel and never really *hear* it. Many times I have heard people say they went to a church for many years and never heard the gospel. Maybe the gospel was not preached there. But such a statement may be more a comment on their spiritual condition than on the spiritual condition of the church. You can "hear" the message but never truly comprehend the grace of God. It is only by God's grace that we understand that not only have all sinned, but *I* have sinned; that God did not just love the world, God loved *me*. That God's amazing grace saved a wretch *like me*.

How did this life-changing Word come to these people? Through the mouth of an ordinary man, Epaphras, who was beloved by his fellow workers, faithful to Christ, and a servant to the church (v. 7). May we all be worthy of such a threefold commendation.

ThinkThrough

When did you truly comprehend the grace of God? How can you pray for others who may have heard but never understood?

Who was your Epaphras who brought to you the Word of life? Who have you been an Epaphras to?

Day 3

Read Colossians 1:9–12

Paul now moves from thanksgiving to petition. Paul always prays for the Colossians, asking "God to fill [them] with the knowledge of his will" (v. 9). By this, Paul does not mean God will tell us who to marry, where to live, or what kind of car to buy. No, Paul is referring to what he has given thanks for earlier, which is the fruit of the gospel in the lives of the Colossians, and that this gospel is changing lives everywhere. This is God's will: the spiritual blessing of all the nations in Christ. He wants us to understand more deeply God's purposes for us and for the world.

This complete knowledge of God's will happens through "all the wisdom and understanding that the Spirit gives" (v. 9). It is a knowledge given to us by the Spirit. Knowing God's will is eminently practical—it is about how we live. Therefore, the purpose of our knowing and doing God's will is that we live a life worthy of the Lord (v. 10). Wouldn't you want someone to say to you, "I have been watching the way you live for the past year and, if you are a Christian, I want to know Christ"? That is a life worthy of the Lord.

Again drawing from Genesis 1, Paul says that this life, which pleases God, expresses itself as we "[bear] fruit in every good work, [and grow] in the knowledge of God" (v. 10). Earlier he spoke of the gospel bearing fruit in the world (v. 6), and now he refers to it in the lives of individual Christians. Lastly, Paul prays that the believers would be empowered to endure and finish the race, continually giving thanks to the Father (vv. 11–12).

The prayers we pray are a good indicator of the extent to which the gospel has transformed our minds. Paul's prayer challenges us to look beyond our present circumstances and our physical needs to the deeper, eternal issues that are on God's heart. Let Paul's prayer transform our prayer lives today.

What does it mean to be filled with the knowledge of God's will? How can you keep on growing in this kind of knowledge?

What does it mean to "not [stop] praying" (v. 9)? Are there any misalignments between the content of our prayers and the kind of prayers God wants us to pray?

Day 4

Read Colossians 1:12–14

In Colossians 1:9–11, we saw how Paul prays for the believers in Colossae. He concluded by praying for their endurance. Now he continues by asking for their perseverance to be marked with joyful thanksgiving. Thus Paul's prayer comes full circle: he begins and ends with thanksgiving. We see Paul displaying what the early Christian theologian St. Augustine termed as one of the great marks of a believer—that is, he or she "is a hallelujah from head to foot."

The Colossians—and we—should be thankful that we have been made fit to inherit the "kingdom of light" (v. 12), the new age of spiritual life and understanding. God's great promise to His people, Israel, was that they would inherit the land of Canaan. But that promise was only a foreshadowing of the true and greater reality. Ultimately, God's promised inheritance was not a piece of land, but the true kingdom in which we enjoy all God's spiritual blessings in Christ. Incredibly, we Gentiles who for so long were outside God's kingdom are now co-heirs.

How is all this possible? Well, look at what happened in the Old Testament. In verses 13 to 14, it appears that Paul has in mind the exodus and the subsequent possession of the promised land. God rescued His people from Pharaoh's dominion of darkness by His mighty hand. This is a picture of the gospel. It is the shadow; the reality is what God has done for us in Jesus. Humanity's true bondage is to sin. The true Pharaoh who enslaves us is the Prince of Darkness; and the true Moses who leads us to our true inheritance is the Lord Jesus. In short, the exodus from Egypt pointed forward to the true exodus from Satan's dominion and into life under the lordship of Jesus. This redemption, the forgiveness of our sins, was accomplished through Jesus' death on the cross.

What a model prayer! This is the kind of prayer God delights in. **This is the prayer God always hears, the kind of prayer that lifts our hearts and minds from our momentary, passing afflictions to the great gospel truths that define who we are and celebrate all God has done and will do for us in Jesus.**

What do you think it means to have God's power in us (v. 11)? Read over Paul's prayer again. How does he see God's power manifesting itself in believers' lives?

What would you say if someone asked you, "What is the gospel?" How has Paul's prayer (vv. 13–14) helped you to clarify what the gospel is?

Day 5

Read Colossians 1:15–16

When a celebrity was asked about what he thought of Jesus, he replied, "A pretty good guy." The banality of that response is astonishing. But even a reply like "a good, moral teacher" is hopelessly inadequate. In some parts of today's world, secularism is triumphing. In other places, millions follow the teachings of those who claim to speak for God. Christians can therefore be tempted to lose heart or to wonder if what we believe is just one among many equally valid, competing truths.

The church in Colossae was a tiny body in an enormous empire. In a world of many gods, the gospel appeared to be just one more barely distinct voice. Paul is writing to bolster the faith of this small group of believers. His prayer for them now morphs into a hymn of praise to the omnipotent Christ.

Look again at how often the word "all" appears in Colossians 1:15–20: Jesus is "the firstborn over all creation. For in him all things were created: things in heaven and on earth, visible and invisible, whether thrones or powers or rulers or authorities; all things have been created through him and for him. He is before all things, and in him all things hold together. And he is the head of the body, the church; he is the beginning and the firstborn from among the dead, so that in everything he might have the supremacy. For God was pleased to have all his fullness dwell in him, and through him to reconcile to himself all things." You see Paul's point: since everything is in Jesus, if you have Jesus, you have everything.

Paul begins by reminding us that every creature on earth was made by and for Jesus—from the toad to the camel, and from the shark to the starling. **Every human being, from paupers to presidents, including you and me, exist for the glory of Jesus. We were given the breath of life to serve Him in this world; and we were given a new breath—the breath of the Holy Spirit—to empower us to live for Him.**

Jesus is not just one other "god" or guru; He is the only God and Lord.

ThinkThrough

What is it about the society in which you live that unsettles your faith? How are Paul's words here a remedy for that?

Who were the thrones, powers, rulers, and authorities of Paul's day that were created for Jesus? How can we see today's rulers, good or bad, serving that same purpose?

Day 6

Read Colossians 1:17–20

Paul continues his breathtaking doxology to Jesus. He reminds us of who Jesus is and of what He has done. **The great theme is Jesus' supremacy over all things, and this supremacy is seen in creation and in redemption.**

Jesus is the eternal Christ. At His incarnation, Jesus became what He was not before—a human being. Christ alone is preexistent, no other person can be given that title. More than that, "in him all things hold together" (v. 17). Not only was the universe created by Him, everything continues to exist because of Him. If it was not for Jesus sustaining all things, the universe would revert to the chaotic state it was in before God first said, "Let there be . . ." (Genesis 1:3). Jesus is supreme.

In verse 18, Paul moves from creation to redemption. Jesus not only brought the *old* creation into being, He has ushered in the *new* creation by His death and resurrection. The new creation begins with people made new. Jesus is their head, because by breaking the bonds of death, He established a new humanity.

And for what purpose? So Jesus might be preeminent over all things. In verse 19, we have one of the most sublime statements about Christ in the whole Bible: all God's power, glory, majesty, wisdom, and grace dwell in Jesus Christ, who is fully man and fully God. Through the divine Son's death and resurrection, God has healed the great rupture that tore His creation apart because of sin. Shalom restored. Peace regained. Enemies reconciled. All through Jesus' blood shed on the cross.

Jesus is the Lord we can entrust our lives to. He is the Lord we must entrust our lives to. There is only one possible response to the Jesus we meet in Colossians 1:15–20: we must worship Him. It is possible that these verses were a song they sang in the early church, because when you see Jesus as He truly is, you can only break out in heartfelt praise and adoration.

ThinkThrough

What are the practical implications for your daily life in believing that Jesus is the Creator, Sustainer, and Redeemer of everything?

Given that most created beings do not worship Jesus, how can Paul say that, "in everything he might have the supremacy"? How does Jesus' supremacy express itself in your life?

Day 7

Read Colossians 1:21–23

How does someone become a Christian? In the next section of this letter, Paul gives two answers to this question. The first is: because of what God has done (vv. 21–23). Having just told us who Jesus is (vv. 15–20), Paul now reminds us how we came to know this Jesus.

In these few verses we have the most amazing summary of the gospel and, indeed, the most compact summary of the whole Christian life. It can be summed up in three very simple words: once . . . but . . . if.

"Once you were alienated" (v. 21). Paul sums up the entire unbelieving world in these words. They are essentially aliens, and it is a relational alienation due to sin. And like all people, we willfully chose to cut ourselves off from God before we were Christians.

"But now he has reconciled you" (v. 22). Enemies are now friends, aliens are now family, all because of Christ's death on the cross. Jesus' death does not just bring us back to God; it also has a future focus—that He might present us holy in His sight, without blemish, free from accusation. The image here is of judgment day, when the bride of Christ is presented to her husband. The question is: are you worthy to enter the kingdom? The psalmist says only the one with clean hands and a pure heart can ascend His holy hill (Psalm 24:4). The good news is that you can confidently reply, "Yes, I am worthy." On that day we will not fear any voice challenging our claim, because Jesus has died for us to make us worthy.

"If you continue in your faith" (v. 23). Of course, our salvation is secure, but we must continue in this gospel. We have been reconciled to God, and we must not go back to being His enemy. His death has made us holy, so we do not deliberately or willfully give ourselves to a life of ungodliness.

This is our spiritual biography: once . . . but . . . if.

"Aliens . . . enemies . . . evil behavior." Is this an overly negative view of the men and women outside of Christ? How can we persuade people that this is a fair and accurate diagnosis of their spiritual condition?

What are the major roadblocks Christians face to continuing in the faith? What can you do to ensure you remain faithful to the end?

Day 8

Read Colossians 1:24–27

How does someone become a Christian? Who brought you to faith—God or your parents; God or your Christian friend; God or an evangelist? Of course, the answer is both. God brought His gospel to you *and* your friend brought the gospel to you. In Colossians 1:21–23, we saw Paul's first answer to this question. He said we are reconciled to God because of what Christ has done. This is both the first and foundational reason for our believing. Now Paul describes how God's saving work was made known to those who were once aliens and enemies.

Paul begins describing his ministry by saying that he fills up what is lacking in Christ's sufferings (v. 24). Is he suggesting that Christ's sufferings were inadequate—that Jesus' death on the cross only paid for some of our sins but not all? Is he saying that he believes his ministry, which is also marked by suffering, somehow atones for the rest of our sins? Of course not!

What was lacking in the process of people coming to faith was someone to bring the good news of salvation to those who needed to hear it. That is what Paul has done. That is what Paul has completed. Paul suffered as an evangelist, but it was all worth it because through his suffering the gospel came to those who needed it.

Paul frequently calls this gospel a "mystery" (v. 26), not because it is cryptic or confusing, but because it is the revelation of all that God promised in the Old Testament. It was "hidden" in all that God did and spoke, but now its reality has been revealed in all that Jesus has done. At the center of this gospel is Jesus Christ—the hope of glory. All of our longings for a glorious future are centered on Jesus.

Bringing the gospel to people is a costly business. Choose ministry, and you have chosen suffering. But oh what riches in the end! **Proclaiming this glorious, hopeful gospel of Christ is something worth suffering and dying for.**

Who brought the good news of Jesus to you? Can you think of what it might have cost them to do this?

What are the "glorious riches of this mystery" (v. 27) that have now been revealed to you and me?

Day 9

Read Colossians 1:28–29

Everything Paul has written since his opening words of thanks has been focused on the godly conduct of the Colossians. He has thanked God for their faith and love; and he has prayed for spiritual wisdom for them so they can live a life worthy of the Lord while patiently enduring trials. The purpose of his "hymn to Christ" is that they may remain established in Him. He now concludes with a wonderful summary of the essence of Christian ministry: the what, the why, and the how.

The *what* of ministry? As verse 28 says, "[Jesus] is the one we proclaim." Our message to the world is not "Make Poverty History," nor "Become a Better You." **Our only message to the world is: "Christ in you, the hope of glory." And thus we warn and teach.** We warn people because our, and their, lives must change from willful rebellion to godly submission. And we teach one another because our ways of thinking must move from being self-centered to God-centered.

Why? So we can be spiritually mature. Paul has already said that the purpose of Christ's death was to present us holy in God's sight, without blemish (v. 22). If I am going to be without blemish then I need to have my blemishes removed. If you have ever had blemishes removed from your skin, then you will know it is painful. But a little pain is worth it to look beautiful. That is exactly what Paul is doing. I do not want to hear sermons that just make me feel good about myself, I need preachers to turn the searchlight of God's Word on my pride, my foolish words, and my selfish desires. God's Word and Spirit have to burn them off to make me to become pleasing in His sight.

How does Paul—and every other teacher—achieve this goal? Through hard work. Paul writes that he labors agonizingly with God's strength by which he is powerfully strengthened (v. 29). Paul sweats and strains to bring the believers to maturity in Christ. Yet all the while, it is the God of all power who is mightily enabling him. And me. And you.

ThinkThrough

What kinds of things should we be warning people against? Why does the New Testament give such an important emphasis to teaching in the church?

Why is the work of ministry so hard?

Day 10

Read Colossians 2:1–5

These wonderful verses conclude the beginning of Paul's letter. He is about to give them godly counsel on enduring as Christians, but first he finishes his lengthy introduction. **In short, he says, "You are fabulously rich in Christ; and don't you let anyone ever tell you otherwise."**

Paul wraps up his introduction by telling them that although he is not physically present, he remains vitally concerned for their spiritual growth. Indeed, he agonizes over them (v. 1), probably in prayer. Who do I agonize over? Well, my children of course. I pray daily for their spiritual growth; and I know many other Christian parents who are in emotional agony over their children's spiritual condition. I constantly agonize over those I love, praying that they will never let go of Jesus.

That is exactly how Paul feels. Although he has not met the believers in Colossae personally, he aches for their growth in spiritual maturity. Specifically, he wants them to know the comfort Christ brings, to be knit together in love, and to know how rich they are to have been given the understanding that Jesus is at the heart of all God's plans for His world (v. 2).

Do you know how rich you are? The richest man is the one who understands truths the world's greatest minds have never understood—that the wise and successful life is the one focused on Christ. The richest woman is the one who grasps that at the heart of all God's plans for the future is Jesus. We may read about CEOs on enormous salaries, but we are richer.

Do not let anyone, inside or outside the church, tell you any differently with "fine-sounding arguments" (v. 4). Do not be swayed by entertaining preachers who tell you that life is all about you and your happiness when it is really about Christ. Do not be charmed by highly qualified teachers who try to persuade you that Christ is anything less than the glorious divine being we met in Colossians 1:15–20. As long as we hold on tight to this Jesus, then our faith will remain strong (v. 5). I pray that everyone, especially those I love, will never let go of Jesus.

In verse 2, Paul longs for the Colossians to display maturity in three areas of their lives. Reflect on what God has done in your life in each of these areas.

What are some of the "fine-sounding arguments" you have heard that try to take your eyes off the Christ revealed to us in the Scriptures?

Day 11

Read Colossians 2:6–7

Paul now gets down to business. Colossians 2:6–7 is really the heart of the epistle. If you always wanted to memorize Colossians, but find four chapters (or 95 verses) too much, then memorize this short passage and you will have the epistle in a nutshell. In these two verses, Paul sums up everything he is about to say.

Verse 6 contains this phrase: "as you received Christ Jesus as Lord." We use the expression "receive Jesus into your heart" as a way of describing how a person becomes a Christian. But Paul means more than that: he is talking about the gospel tradition of the crucified, risen, and exalted Christ that has been passed on. It is the responsibility of every generation to receive, embrace, and then pass on, without any change or dilution, these wonderful truths about Christ and His salvation.

The first name used for Christians was "the Way" (Acts 9:2). This is fitting since Christians, who have received Jesus into their hearts—both then and now—are to continually walk in Him. **Paul's one command here is to live this faith out.** In the rest of the letter, Paul will describe the road we walk on.

How do we keep on walking? We must walk with our roots deep in Jesus. We do so by building ourselves up and becoming mature in Jesus, being strengthened in the faith we were taught (v. 7). In other words, by constantly growing in our understanding of the gospel truths that first brought us to Jesus. That is why the best sermons tell me nothing new. They may give me a new appreciation for an old truth, or apply a truth of Scripture in an insightful way, but they keep bringing me back to Jesus.

For the same reason, we flirt with spiritual danger if we attend a church that is not gospel-focused in its teaching; and we stunt our spiritual growth if we feed our minds on talks and books that talk too much about us and too little about Jesus.

When Jesus fills our hearts and minds, and we become firmly rooted in His truth, then our mouths will be full of thanksgiving.

How did you receive Christ? How has your understanding of Jesus and your love for Him grown since then?

What kind of Christian teaching do you fill your mind with? How is it keeping you established in the faith and growing in maturity?

Day 12

Read Colossians 2:8–10

We all want to remain firmly grounded in our faith, continually following Jesus. However, there are some distractions that may derail us. In Colossians 2:8–10, Paul warns us against three spiritual dangers—all to do with ways of thinking.

The first danger is found in verse 8. Paul warns us against being hijacked by "deceptive philosophy." These are teachings that will lead us away from Christ. They are based on human traditions, which are ways of thinking that do not have Christ at their center. Paul also calls these kinds of ideas "elemental spiritual forces of this world" (v. 8). They are the kinds of philosophy that keep us focused on the things of this world. What does that look like today? It is the foolish belief that only what you can see, hear, smell, and touch is real. It is the empty philosophy which says, "Eat, drink, and be merry, for tomorrow you die." It is the blinkered worldview that says you can live a successful and godly life and not have Jesus Christ at its center.

Why are these ways of looking at life and the world so empty? It is simply because all the fullness of God dwells bodily in Christ (v. 9). If all God's fullness is in Christ, then there is none left over to indwell anyone or anything else. **Therefore, any worldview that does not recognize the centrality of Christ is distorted.** It also means that if we walk away from Jesus, then we walk away from God.

We now live in this Christ. This Jesus is the head over every authority. Pilate thought he had the power to decide whether Christ lived or died, but Jesus told him otherwise (John 19:10–11). Satan thought he had won a victory by engineering Christ's death, but God had ordained otherwise (Colossians 2:15). Even earthly authorities who think they call the shots when it comes to who and how their citizens should worship, ultimately serve the One who has been given all authority.

ThinkThrough

What are some of the worldly ways of thinking that threaten to hijack your faith? How can you guard yourself from being deceived by foolish philosophies?

What are the practical implications of recognizing that Christ is the head over every power and authority?

Day 13

Read Colossians 2:11–15

Dead, buried, and risen. This is Jesus' story—and ours! Paul now graphically reminds us of the fullness we have in Christ (v. 10). Unusually, verse 11 seems to use circumcision as a metaphor for Jesus' death: His body was slashed and stripped naked on the cross. **Because we are in Christ, when He died, we died; and when He was buried, we were buried with Him. His subsequent resurrection is our rising to new life.** This death won our forgiveness and no one can condemn us any longer (v. 14), not even the devil.

On one level, Jesus' entire ministry was a battle against Satan, especially His death on the cross. What appeared to be Satan's great victory was actually his terrible defeat. To illustrate that, Paul selects an image that would be very familiar to his first-century readers (v. 15). When a Roman general won a great victory, it was the custom for him to publicly humiliate the enemy army by dragging them, in chains, through the streets of Rome while the crowd jeered at them.

Afterwards, the defeated general would be publicly executed.

This is exactly what Jesus has done with the forces of darkness. By His death and resurrection, our conquering King has stripped dignity and power from the forces of darkness and has set His people free.

The defeated foe whispers, "You're not worthy," and, "God will never forgive you for that." Don't listen to his lies. You have died with Christ! And don't let the devil convince you that death is the end. You have risen with Christ!

As Martin Luther wrote,

> And though this world, with devils filled, should threaten to undo us,
> We will not fear, for God hath willed His truth to triumph through us;
> The Prince of Darkness grim, we tremble not for him;
> His rage we can endure, for lo, his doom is sure,
> One little word shall fell him.

Count how many times Paul writes "in him" or "in Christ" in these first two chapters. How do you respond to this understanding of all you have in Christ?

What are some of the devil's lies that can unsettle our faith? How can the truth of verse 15 affect our life and thinking as Christians?

Day 14

Read Colossians 2:16–17

I once heard someone who had a near-death experience speak in church. He shared, "I thought I was a Christian before, but now I'm more of a Christian." I thought to myself, how could you become more of a Christian? It is like an expectant mother saying, "I'm more pregnant." Her pregnancy may be more advanced, but you are either pregnant or not pregnant. Likewise, you are either in Christ or not in Christ.

In Colossians 2:10, Paul says, "in Christ you have been brought to fullness." Not 25 percent, or even 99 percent, but fullness. We have been "made . . . alive with Christ"(v. 13), not left hovering between life and death. You get the picture? Done. Finished. Complete.

In this next section (Colossians 2:16–19), Paul addresses the second danger to our growing in Christ. Apparently there were some Jewish Christians who were accusing the Gentile believers of not being fully or properly Christian because they were not keeping the Jewish food and drink laws or the religious festivals (v. 16). Of course, there are certain willful, sinful behaviors that do disqualify

unrepentant practitioners from God (see 1 Corinthians 6:9–10), but that is not what Paul is talking about here.

Paul briefly explains where these judgmental Christians have gone wrong (v. 17). They have forgotten that these Jewish laws were only the foreshadowing; the reality is Christ. You and I belong to this new age. Do not let anyone try to take you back to a bygone age.

You simply cannot say to someone, "I recognize that you are fully 'in Christ,' but you cannot fully belong in my church because you do not keep the Sabbath the way we do, or eat or drink what we do, or dress for church the way we do." And so on.

Today we are reminded that no one is a slave, or second-rate, in God's household of sons and daughters; we are all equally and fully His children. There is no "next level of spiritual power" or "deeper spiritual intimacy with Jesus." We have already been given all the riches that God has for us in Christ.

Are there certain behaviors that do cut us off from Christ and His body? How can we discern what is essential for maintaining fellowship and what is not essential?

How should we respond when we believe we are being judged for a belief or behavior that is a matter of Christian freedom?

Day 15

Read Colossians 2:18–19

Paul now gives his third and final warning against listening to those who try to disqualify believers because of beliefs or behaviors the gospel does not condemn.

Essentially he says, "Do not let anyone . . . disqualify you" (v. 18). Or make you feel inferior. Or make you feel like you are missing out and not really part of God's people. The particular problems Paul is addressing are a little hard to tie down. There were some critics who wanted to disqualify the Colossians because they lacked humility. Of course, humility is a wonderful virtue (see Colossians 3:12), but there is also a false kind of humility. This comes from the kind of people who deny themselves things and then make others feel guilty because they do not. It is fine to fast or decide to give half of our income to world missionary work, but we aren't to disqualify others on that basis because they've made other choices.

Paul then talks about the worship of angels. This may refer to some who claimed to have enjoyed dreams and visions in which they saw things that only the angels in worship have seen. Such people, then and now, go into great detail about what they have seen. Sadly, they then arrogantly make the rest of us feel inferior because we have not experienced the same. Paul is not against dreams and visions—he had both—but he did not disqualify others who had not experienced those things.

In verse 19, Paul turns the tables on the disqualifiers. They were trying to disqualify others by their judgmental attitudes when, in fact, they were the ones out of touch and in spiritual danger. They had begun to put more confidence in their own dreams, visions, and experiences than in the Lord Jesus and all He has done for us.

Sadly, it is all too common to hear Christians advocating a super spirituality, such as: just claim this promise or pray this prayer or complete this course, and spiritual riches undreamed of will be yours. Paul says we should not be fooled by them. Stay with Christ; stay with His body.

ThinkThrough

Have other Christians ever insisted that you need to have had a similar experience of God as them or claimed you are missing out? How should we respond to such people?

Are there times when you have felt unworthy as a Christian? What comfort and challenge does the teaching of Colossians bring at such moments?

Day 16

Read Colossians 2:20–23

A girl recently began attending the church of a friend of mine. She was stunned that her new church allowed people to give freewill offerings. She asked my friend, "What are the 'laws of giving' in this church?" In her previous church, members of the congregation were asked to give a specified percentage every week, a special offering at the end of the year, and an offering to the missions fund. It may be good to set a standard for how much to give, but ultimately God wants cheerful givers who decide in their own hearts what to give (2 Corinthians 9:7). This is freedom, not law.

In Colossians 2:11–19, Paul has just reminded the Colossians of the freedom they have in Christ. He instructed them not to let other people judge or disqualify them by imposing their own rules; even rules of value cannot be imposed on others as requirements for fellowship. Moreover, these rules don't usually lead to godliness.

For Paul, living by such rules is another feature of the old life, the "elemental spiritual forces of this world" (v. 20), which we are already dead to. Paul urges us not to submit to rules based on things that do not last. What we eat or drink, the clothes we wear, the days we celebrate—these are all passing away. Moreover, these rules are all merely human requirements. These rules appear wise and spiritual, but they fail to restrain the flesh. You can keep a law of tithing but still be greedy and stingy. You can avoid certain foods and still be a glutton.

The other great danger in living a life based on rules is that it can make us legalistic and judgmental. "I must have an hour-long daily quiet time" can easily become "You must have an hour-long daily quiet time."

How then should we live? **We try to live a disciplined life and pursue that which promotes godliness. But we must continue to come back to the gospel, reminding ourselves that we have died and risen again with Christ—the true power and motivation for godly living**. Go back and read Paul's prayer again (Colossians 1:9–14).

ThinkThrough

In the next two chapters, Paul will give some rules for the Colossians to follow (e.g., Colossians 3:5,18–22; 4:2). What is the difference between these rules and what Paul is warning us against here?

What is it about the gospel Paul describes in Colossians that promotes godliness in the lives of those who embrace it?

Day 17

Read Colossians 3:1–4

Old habits die hard. A few years ago a friend of mine moved from a city with a very high crime rate to the relative safety of Melbourne, Australia. In her previous home she used to chain her car to a tree when she went out shopping, and they had three locks on every door in their house. Having moved to her new home, what does my friend do now? She still gets anxious when she leaves the house and keeps multiple locks on her doors. My friend needs to realize she has left the old life behind. A new way of living will require a new way of thinking.

Paul is about to encourage the Colossians to live differently, but first they need to think differently. He reminds them, again, that they have died and risen with Christ (vv. 1–3). Therefore, they should set their minds on things above. If we are going to live faithful, constructive lives on earth, our minds must always be in heaven. **Paul is essentially saying, "Look to Christ. Seek to please Him. Seek the reward He gives. Seek His forgiveness when you fail. Seek His power in your weakness."**

Occasionally, we do not feel like we have died to our old life and entered into a whole new existence with Jesus. Sometimes, we may look, feel, and even behave as we did before. But do not be fooled; our true life is "hidden with Christ" (v. 3). We may not always be able to sense our connection to Jesus, but the reality is that we belong to Him; and one day everyone will see our true, glorious identity when Jesus comes again. Until then, we need to keep reminding ourselves of who we are.

While the faith of some people is too intellectual and theoretical, we must never despise our minds. How we think affects how we behave. My friend needs to remind herself daily of her new home. She needs to set her mind there. Then she will be afraid no longer and will experience the freedom that is hers. I daily remind myself where I live: in Christ—once dead, now risen and alive.

ThinkThrough

What do you think it means to "set your minds on things above" (v. 2)? What practical steps can you take to do that?

What are some of the old habits from your past life that you find hard to let go of? How can an understanding of what Jesus has done for us, and who we are in Him, help us to change?

Day 18

Read Colossians 3:5–7

Like night and day, or black and white, in Colossians 3:5–7, Paul marks a stark contrast between a life set on the things above and one absorbed with the things of the world.

"Therefore" (v. 5), or in other words, since you have died and risen with Christ, here is the kind of life you must live. Firstly, Paul gives us the "Don'ts" (vv. 5–11) and then the "Do's" (vv. 12–17). In this first section (vv. 5–11), he addresses two enormous issues: our speech and our sexuality.

Regarding sexuality, some people may say, "But I just can't control myself!" Yet Paul replies, "Yes, you can." You have the power to say "no" to destructive sexual desires. One does not need to be too precise as to the distinctions between impurity, lust, evil passions, and covetousness. Paul is just covering all the bases. In short, he is cataloging any sexual behavior that is conducted outside the one-man–one-woman, faithful, lifelong marriage union.

It goes without saying that our fallen human sexuality exercises an enormous pull on us. This "war within" rages in the minds and hearts of many Christians. Indeed, Paul would say that, apart from our empowering union with Christ, we would otherwise be largely impotent in this battle.

Because of Christ, we can say "no" to sinful behaviors. Paul does not ever give the churches a command without also giving them the spiritual resources to keep it. The Colossians themselves are a living testimony to that, as they "used to walk in these ways" (v. 7). But they do not any longer, because God has radically transformed them. This should be our testimony too.

We must say "no" to sin. "Because of these [sins], the wrath of God is coming" (v. 6). Therefore, we must quickly "put to death" (v. 5) whatever belongs to our earthly nature. When it comes to immorality, there can be no compromise. We must not delude ourselves. We have been rescued from the dominion of darkness (Colossians 1:13), so we cannot behave like we still live in darkness. We are strengthened with all power according to His glorious might (v. 11), so that we can live God-honoring, countercultural lives of sexual purity.

What are some of the sexual struggles men and women face in your context? In the light of Paul's words here, what counsel can you bring?

If people require the empowering presence of God to bring permanent life changes, how can we help those who are not Christians in their struggle against sexual addictions? How should we be speaking into the non-Christian culture that rejects biblical notions of sex and marriage?

Day 19

Read Colossians 3:8–11

The Christian life is like a wardrobe. In any wardrobe there are both old and new clothes. My wife likes to throw out many of my old clothes because they no longer fit, they now look silly on me, or they are simply worn out. My problem is I get too attached to my old clothes. However, some of them just have to go.

This is exactly what Paul says in Colossians 3:5–11. He has been describing our new life, and like our old clothes, there are certain behaviors that do not "fit" anymore and have to go. Paul has already described the transformation that should take place in our sexual behavior (vv. 5–7), now he talks about the radical change in the things we say (vv. 8–10).

Moses told Israel to take to heart all the words he had spoken to them because "they are your life" (Deuteronomy 32:46–47). We live or die by the words we hear and speak. Therefore, we must speak life-giving, life-enhancing words. Paul gives us five examples of the kind of words that wound, spoil, and destroy. There is the seething hatred or simmering wrath, which then may express itself in fits of rage. Then there is the malicious destruction of someone's reputation and character; and fourthly, there is blasphemy or slander—those words that dishonor God by demeaning those made in His image. Finally, we must put away the gutter talk that soils and pollutes.

In a community renewed by the truth of the gospel, we should not lie to one another (v. 9). We must avoid the lie that, since we are forgiven, what we do with our bodies or our tongues does not matter. And the same goes for the lie that God will not hold us accountable for every careless word spoken.

We have changed clothes. We have a whole new wardrobe. We are now part of a new community that God is daily renewing. It is a community of purity and truth where there are no barriers or distinctions—no "them" and "us" (v. 11). Let us resolve today, and every day, to throw away those inappropriate old clothes.

ThinkThrough

If we find ourselves surrounded by people who continually speak unkind, impure, or untrue words, how can we learn to discipline ourselves in the things that we say?

What are some of the ungodly distinctions that sometimes exist in your church? How does the gospel help us to look at one another with new eyes?

Day 20

Read Colossians 3:12–14

Let us return to the wardrobe. We have just taken off, and hopefully thrown away, the old clothes. Now let us dress ourselves in garments of life and beauty.

I do hope you understand—because Paul has been repeating it constantly—that the power to live the Christian life comes from outside of us. It comes from our union with Christ. His death to sin was our death to sin; His rising to life was our resurrection. We are not what we were before: we are being remade into something completely new. This is not moralism. Moralism is: do it yourself. Moralism says, "Just do it! Change yourself." **Christian living is: remember what God has done for you in Christ, and remember who you are in Christ.**

Paul begins this section with, "Therefore [because you're being renewed in God's image], as God's chosen people [that's who you are], holy and dearly loved [set apart by God's love lavished upon you], clothe yourselves with . . ." (v. 12). All that Paul is calling us to do springs from our understanding of who we are in Christ.

Since we are now "in Christ," it is not surprising that the clothes we put on must bear the image of Christ. Paul calls us to be compassionate like Jesus, who had compassion on the crowds that were harassed and helpless. We are to be kind, humble, gentle, and patient like Jesus, who said, "Come to me, all you who are weary and burdened . . . for I am gentle and humble in heart" (Matthew 11:28–29). We are to "forgive as the Lord forgave you" (Colossians 3:13). Above all, we must put on love, "as I have loved you" (John 13:34). In short, we are to be clothed with Christ-likeness. Of course, God will definitely do this in the lives of those He is remaking in His Son's image.

Sadly, too often Christians are taught to rely on themselves to change, instead of on Christ. We need to be reminded to focus on what God has done for us in Christ and who we are in Him. Only then will our hearts and lives be transformed—from the inside out.

Reflect upon your own Christian gatherings. Do they display the kind of conduct Paul describes here? How can we see our churches grow in this kind of Christ-likeness?

Which of the Christian virtues that Paul mentions here do you particularly struggle with? What would moralism say to you? How does the gospel transform you?

Day 21

Read Colossians 3:15–17

Living life as a Christian expresses itself in our daily interactions, as well as when we meet together as God's people in our weekly church gatherings. Paul now mentions three features of our life as Christian communities.

Firstly, he exhorts us to be people of peace (v. 15). Our war with God is over because Jesus has "[made] peace through his blood" (Colossians 1:20). This peace then floods our hearts and heals our relationships. We no longer live in fear and guilt before God, because we know that we are forgiven and we are His children. Therefore, our relationships must be marked by forgiveness and the absence of hostility.

Paul then exhorts us to be thankful (3:15). Hearts full of God's peace should be hearts full of thanks.

Finally, "the message of Christ," the gospel and all the teachings and doctrines of and about Jesus, should lavishly fill our communal lives (v. 16). We teach and admonish. We bring to God's people new insights or fresh reminders of what God has done for us in Christ; and we correct wrong ideas, wrong attitudes, and wrong behaviors.

But then the passage takes a surprising twist. How does Christ's Word dwell in His people? I would have said something like this: "Teaching and admonishing one another with regular Bible studies, daily quiet times, and hearing lots of great sermons." Of course, these are all very important, but Paul exhorts us to sing (v. 16)! We are to sing the psalms of the Psalter, "hymns" (probably the other songs of the Bible), and "songs from the Spirit"— all those songs, old and new, inspired by the Spirit. **Singing has always been a major vehicle for conveying God's truth. That's why Paul exhorts us to sing to one another.** It remains a very important dimension of the teaching ministry of the church today. There is a horizontal dimension to our singing: we sing to one another; and there is also a vertical dimension to our singing: we sing to the Lord.

I was in a church recently where we sang for twenty minutes, and none of the songs spoke of the gospel. They neither edified the body nor glorified God our Savior. Let us sing instead as the Scriptures exhort us to sing.

ThinkThrough

Reflect upon your church experience. Is peace a feature of your life as a Christian community? In the light of what Paul says in Colossians 3:15–17, how can we bring healing and reconciliation when relationships are damaged or broken in our midst?

Think about the singing in your church. How are the songs deepening your understanding of the gospel? Does your church sing "psalms, hymns, and songs from the Spirit"?

Day 22

Read Colossians 3:18–19

There is much confusion in today's society about marriage. In the world today, many are promoting same-sex marriages. Others see marriage as outdated, even oppressive; not to mention the general public acceptance of divorce and cohabitation before marriage. We are moving very quickly away from the biblical understanding of marriage.

Since the beginning of chapter three, Paul has been describing the kind of life that is worthy of the Lord. Now he shifts his attention to the home, because this is the true testing ground for living out the values of the new life.

Paul begins with God's command to husbands and wives. Wives must submit to their husbands (v. 18). These words seem galling to many, but in our relationships, the Bible consistently calls us to submit to others: to God, the governing authorities, pastors, masters or employers, elders, and, indeed, to one another (Ephesians 5:21). In each case we submit to those whose responsibility it is to care for us. Therefore, the wife is to submit to her husband because he is concerned for her welfare and will deny his own desires to satisfy hers. The wife will joyfully submit to a husband who is living the kind of life Paul has just described: clothing himself with humility, compassion, kindness, and love.

Tragically, too many husbands have abused their role. Paul reminds them to love their wives and not become harsh or bitter towards them (v. 19). There is no place for bullying in any of our relationships, especially marriage.

The two commands go hand in hand. The husband needs to so love his wife that she will delight in submitting to him; and the wife needs to so joyfully serve her husband that he in turn will find delight in loving her.

This is the proper order God has ordained for godly marriages. And it works, because it is also the pathway to a happy marriage. In a world with so much pain and brokenness in marriage, a marriage that lives out God's command is a powerful testimony to what God has ordained as best for humanity.

Why do we often react against the word *submit*? What is the biblical idea of submission, and why does it see submission as important for healthy relationships?

If you are married, how can you better express these godly values of submission and love in your relationship?

Day 23

Read Colossians 3:20–21

t is astonishing, given all the books that have been written on marriage and raising children, that Paul says everything he wants to say in forty-two words in the original Greek text! Presumably, he's focusing on key issues.

Paul's command to children to obey their parents echoes the fifth commandment to "honor your father and your mother" (Exodus 20:12). In the Old Testament, to disobey one's parents was tantamount to disobeying God, which was as serious as treason or idolatry. In fact, Paul saw increasing disobedience to parents as one of the signs of the end times (2 Timothy 3:1–2). A child here does not just mean a young boy or girl. One commentator points out that in Paul's time, a father had authority in the home until he was 60 years of age or passed away. But the outworking of a parent's authority changes as the children mature. Children are to respect their parents "in everything" (Colossians 3:20); but as they become less dependent on their parents and, in particular, move away from home, the degree and extent of the obedience required is less. Still, respect and care for one's parents is a lifelong obligation, though it will express itself differently.

Is it not amazing that, of all the advice Paul could give, Paul's one word of exhortation to parents is: do not embitter or discourage your children (v. 21). In the ancient world, fathers had absolute power over their children, even over life and death. Today, parents still have tremendous physical, emotional, and psychological power over their children, and this power can be dreadfully abused.

Therefore, do not exasperate your children. Parents can commit this mistake in various ways: by showing favoritism; giving harsh comments without reasons and without reminders of their love; punishing with unreasonable anger; causing embarrassment; or expecting perfection.

Research from around the world is extensive and overwhelming. Stable, God-centered families are good for society. By every measure children do better in this environment. **When God, who ordained family life, gives instructions on how it ought to operate, He must be listened to because this is the way to life, love, and happiness.**

How all-encompass-ing do you think Paul's command is to children to obey their parents in everything? Are there situations when a child, whether young or old, should not give complete obedience to a parent?

Can you think of any other ways that parents can embitter or discourage their children? Conversely, how can parents positively build up the lives of their children?

Day 24

Read Colossians 3:22–4:1

How much does knowledge of the coming judgment influence your Christian behavior now? **In Paul's final piece of advice to families, slaves, and masters, the motivation he gives for obedience is that everyone will have to answer to the Lord (v. 24).**

Paul gives a surprising amount of space to addressing slaves, especially when we recall how brief his comments have been to all the others in the household. In fact, most of the space is taken up in developing the reason why slaves ought to be subject to their masters. I suspect this is because Paul recognizes that while our levels of submission are different, we all have people to whom we are accountable.

Paul's command is that the slave should be wholeheartedly obedient and not be the kind of worker who works hard when the boss is around, but slacks off when he is away (v. 22). Why should workers do this? Well, because they fear the Lord! On the one hand, there is the earnest expectation of receiving a heavenly reward for their obedience, and on the other, there is the terror of the loss of that reward (vv. 24–25). After all, "It is the Lord Christ you are serving" (v. 24). Our real master is Jesus. Therefore, if you think you are deceiving your earthly master, remember the one you are really trying to deceive is the Lord Jesus.

Paul then rounds off this warning by reminding his audience of a great biblical principle: God shows no partiality (v. 25). God will not say, "Oh, you were a lazy, slothful, deceitful Christian; well, that's okay." No, God is impartial and He will always punish deliberate, persistent disobedience, no matter who commits it.

When Paul turns to the masters, he similarly bases his command on the certainty of judgment day. Masters are to treat their slaves, or employers are to treat their employees, fairly because they have a master in heaven. Masters may be the head of their earthly households, but they are still answerable to the Lord in heaven.

There is a banner over my life: "Judgment Day Integrity." We live now in the light of that day. Let us work out our salvation with "fear and trembling" (Philippians 2:12).

How much does the reality of the coming judgment influence your Christian life? If perfect love casts out fear, why does Paul frequently exhort us to fear the Lord?

What is an employee's obligation to a boss who is a bully or unjust? How should Christian bosses deal with lazy or troublesome employees?

Read Colossians 4:2–4

love to listen to godly people pray. Just as I learn from the wisdom of gifted preachers, I learn from the wisdom and experience of faithful, diligent "pray-ers." Often I am rebuked for my small-minded and egocentric prayers. I need a bigger landscape to pray over. Paul gives me that landscape.

We have already seen the eternal issues that set Paul's prayer agenda (Colossians 1:3–14). Paul now gives us the how and what of prayer.

How should we pray? Regularly. It is something we must be deeply committed to. A wise Christian sets regular times for prayer and keeps to them. Watchfully. We must be alert to the issues we should be praying about, especially salvation issues. Thankfully. Just count how many times Paul mentions being thankful in this letter (Colossians 1:3,12; 2:7; 3:15–17). The first words I utter when I pray are "Thank you."

And what does Paul pray for? Yes, he asks for prayer for himself (and his co-workers like Epaphras), but it is personal prayer for the sake of others. He wants an open door, but not to his prison cell (although, I dare say, his friends were praying for that). Instead, it is for opportunities to preach the gospel (4:3). And, of course, he also wants the doors of people's hearts to be opened. The message he longs to proclaim is the one the Colossians heard from Epaphras, and have been reminded of in this letter—it is the soaring truth that, from eternity, God has planned the salvation of Jews and Gentiles through His Son, the Lord Jesus. And Paul prays that he might "proclaim [this message] clearly, as [he] should" (v. 4). Paul desires his public proclamation to bring true knowledge and understanding of what Christ has done.

What do you pray for? We are to make all our requests known to God, both the small and great. But too often the "smaller issues" take much of the time, and we neglect the big issues that are on God's heart. **Let us be big "pray-ers" who pray, like Paul, big prayers.**

What have you learned about prayer from others? What changes could you make in your life so that you are praying more regularly, watchfully, and thankfully?

To what extent do issues of eternity drive the content of your prayers? What kind of balance do you think there should be in your prayers between the earthly and spiritual, temporal and eternal?

Day 26

Read Colossians 4:5–6

live in a big city, and right in the heart of that city. My wife and I love it. We love the hustle and bustle, and having people all around us. We live next to our church—a beacon of light in a city of people who give little thought to Jesus. Your situation may be very similar.

How should we live as Christians in a non-Christian world? We do not lock ourselves away in monasteries. We also do not cut ourselves off from the people around us. Paul's last piece of counsel to the Colossians is how we are to live with "outsiders." He says two things: walk and talk.

Paul has already talked about walking the Christian life (Colossians 1:10; 2:6), and now he tells us to walk and act wisely with those outside of Christ (Colossians 4:5). We have seen that there are really only two kinds of people in the world: those in Christ, and those "outside." Paul has repeatedly spoken about wisdom (Colossians 1:9, 28; 2:3; 3:16), and we need it particularly in our interactions with outsiders. We need to ensure our lives match our confession. We need to know when to compromise and when to stand our ground, making the best use of our time. It is like seeing a sign outside a shop: "Massive Sale! Last Days!" In other words, rush in now because the time is short. **That is Paul's point: Jesus is coming soon; do not mess around with your conduct; live godly lives before outsiders!**

Next, Paul tells us to talk with speech full of God's grace, being winsome and compelling (4:6). Note: Paul is not telling us to get out in the streets and start evangelizing (although that would be a very good thing). We cannot all do that. But we can always give an answer to those who are searching for one. All around us, and especially during tough times, people want to know the answers to the big questions. What is life about? Is there something after death? Where is God? What do you Christians believe? We should pray for these often surprising opportunities. And be ready. Know what and why you believe.

ThinkThrough

How important is wisdom in our interactions with non-Christians?

Can you think of times in your life when you have had an opportunity to talk about the Lord Jesus with someone? Do you feel prepared to give answers to questions that could lead you to explaining the gospel? How can you equip yourself better for such occasions?

Read Colossians 4:7–18

Paul bids farewell at this point, with a treasure of spiritual nuggets hidden in his departing words.

Paul first mentions two men well known to the Colossians: Tychicus and Onesimus (vv. 7–9). And look at their commendations! Paul values Tychicus as a faithful servant and fellow slave for Christ and His people. What a wonderful epitaph! We will read much more of Onesimus later. Paul is sending them back to give the Colossians an update on his situation.

Paul then brings greetings from three Jews and three Gentiles who are with him (vv. 10–14). Tragically, of all the Jewish fellow workers who once labored and traveled with Paul, only Aristarchus, Mark, and Jesus Justus have remained his faithful companions through all he has endured. Do not be surprised when people who were once zealous for ministry walk away, like Demas, who later abandoned Paul. Though Demas was serving with Paul faithfully at the time when Colossians was written, sadly there will be another reference to him in a later letter of Paul's (2 Timothy 4:10). But how encouraging it is to see Mark's name in this list. Twelve years earlier he had "deserted them" (Acts 15:36-41), but now he is restored and laboring for the gospel. All these men were working agonizingly for the maturity of the Colossians.

Thirdly, Paul sends greetings to the church in Laodicea, next door to Colossae, and specifically to a church in the home of a woman named Nympha (v. 15). Christians often met in people's homes. Paul mentions a letter he wrote to the Laodiceans (v. 16), which has presumably been lost. Paul may have been in prison, but he did not waste his time there. He continued to pray for these churches and pastor them through his letters. God has preserved a number of these letters so that we too can grow to maturity.

Finally, Paul picks up the pen from his secretary and says a goodbye filled with grace (v. 18).

What a wonderful letter. It soars with Christ-glorifying truth that influences us in every area of our lives. For 2,000 years, the words of Colossians have anchored the faith of those who have received Jesus. **Let us continue to heed its message: "So then, just as you received Christ Jesus as Lord, continue to live your lives in him, rooted and built up in him, strengthened in the faith as you were taught, and overflowing with thankfulness" (Colossians 2:6–7).**

From these verses, what picture can you draw about the character of Christian ministry?

Write your epitaph. How would you like people to sum up your life in twenty words or less?

Day 28

Read Philemon 1:1–7

Philemon is a very different kind of letter from Paul. It is not written to a church like Colossians or Romans, and it is not written to a co-worker like Timothy or Titus. It is written to a particular individual in a church, to address a very specific and personal pastoral issue. What this issue is will become clear as the letter proceeds. But while specific to the church leader Philemon, the letter gives us a wonderful insight into the dynamic, transforming character of Christian fellowship, and the pastoral heart and approach of the great apostle and church planter Paul.

Paul and Timothy bring greetings to Philemon, a woman called Apphia, (perhaps his wife), Archippus (either a key church member or perhaps even Philemon's son), and to the church (vv. 1–2). Interesting. In many ways this is a personal letter addressing a personal issue, but Paul expected the letter to be read out to the whole church. The church met in Philemon's home, so they would know Onesimus, the man who, in a moment, would be revealed as the reason Paul is writing. **While not all things personal should be shared with the church, this letter is a wonderful picture of true Christian fellowship.** We weep and laugh together. We bear each other's burdens. We pray for each other and encourage one another. Therefore, it is appropriate in this situation that Philemon's spiritual brothers and sisters listen in while Paul addresses him personally.

As Paul prays for Philemon, we see the caliber of the man. Philemon is full of faith and love for both Christ and His people; his life is a refreshing blessing for the believers (vv. 4–7). And Paul wants Philemon's partnership in the faith to be effective (v. 6). Of course, Paul says this knowing the request he is about to make of Philemon. When someone lets you down, it tests a relationship. Onesimus has deeply wronged Philemon. His return will test Philemon's understanding of true Christian fellowship; and Paul prays he might know all the good that God wants him to do, for Jesus' sake.

ThinkThrough

What is your experience of fellowship in your church? Are you in relationships with others that are transparent, supportive, and include mutual accountability? What can we do to deepen the fellowship in our churches?

Read Philemon 1:8–16

The big stick or the gentle word? How do we influence people to do what is right? There is, of course, a time and place for both. But as the apostle Paul addresses a delicate pastoral problem, we see his preferred method of influence.

In Philemon 1:8–16, Paul spells out the issue: Philemon's slave, Onesimus, had run away but, by God's sovereign will, had met Paul and been converted. He has been of tremendous personal help to Paul, and it is clear that Paul would like to keep Onesimus with him, but he cannot. It would be illegal to keep someone else's slave and a serious breach of fellowship with his dear brother Philemon. Thus he sends him home. Can you image the impact when the newly converted Onesimus first turned up at the church in Philemon's home?

Paul wants Philemon to receive Onesimus back, but as much more than a slave. He is now a brother in Christ, equal in standing before their Master in heaven. Look at how Paul tackles this problem. He does not throw his apostolic weight around.

Rather, he exhorts and appeals. This is a principle by which he consistently conducts his relationships with the churches and his fellow workers. Paul wants voluntary decisions (v. 14). He wants people to be persuaded by his arguments, which are rooted in the gospel. And the gospel spells freedom. Paul wants to help people to discover their Christian freedom; not bind them with more rules.

Finally, because people know the gospel and have the indwelling Spirit, Paul is convinced they will know "every good thing" (Philemon 1:6) they should do and have the desire to do it (v. 21).

In the church there is always the temptation to be authoritarian and heavy-handed. That is not Paul's way, unless it is a matter of spiritual life and death. A runaway slave will not be an issue we come up against, but whatever problems we do face in the church, we can find resolutions as we examine them in the light of the gospel.

ThinkThrough

The gospel transforms relationships. Think about your own personal relationships and the relationships in your church. How have you seen the gospel make an impact there? Where is there room for more growth?

When is it appropriate to give commands and use "the big stick," and when should we bring a gentler word of exhortation?

How can open, honest sharing be abused in a church? How can we be wise in what we share publicly in the gathering of Christians?

Read Philemon 1:17–25

It's easy to love people who already love you (Matthew 5:46)—that's not a big deal and no mark of the presence of the Spirit among God's people. But to love people who have seriously wronged you makes the world sit up and take notice.

In this final section of his letter, Paul makes explicit what he wants from Philemon.

Onesimus has three strikes against him. Strike one: as a slave, he was useless (v. 11). Strike two: he ran away. Strike three: he probably stole from his master (v. 18). Who would even want such a slave back?

But look at what Paul asks of Philemon: "Welcome him as you would welcome me" (v. 17). Receive this slave with the same delight, respect, and kindness that you would your apostle and father in the faith. Indeed, Paul is hopeful that Philemon might soon have an opportunity to do that very thing (v. 22). It is an incredible request, but a true mark of genuine faith and fellowship, because the Onesimus who is returning is Philemon's brother in Christ. Their relationship simply cannot be the same as before.

But let us not underestimate the magnitude of Paul's request.

Forgiveness is costly and sometimes painful. Yet Paul can write that he is "confident of [Philemon's] obedience" (v. 21). Paul knows Philemon's godly character (v. 7) and therefore expects that his friend will want to do what is right. And who knows, perhaps even set Onesimus free or return him to Paul.

According to church tradition, a bishop of Ephesus at the turn of the first century was called Onesimus. Coincidence? Perhaps. But we can be sure that the preservation of this letter is testimony to the fact that, in this particular case, God's people behaved like the redeemed and reconciling community they are.

This brief letter is an inspiring window into the transforming power of the gospel in the life of the church! It shows broken relationships being restored and carries the expectation that God's people will do what is right as they grow strong in Christ.

Your church and mine should be no different, for we have the same Lord and the same Spirit.

Why is Paul so confident that Philemon will do what he asks? Can we have the same confidence about people in our churches?

Think about your church. What evidence do you see of the redeemed and reconciling community at work in the life of your church?

NOTES

NOTES

NOTES

NOTES

NOTES

NOTES

Our Daily Bread
Ministries®

IT'S ABOUT GOD'S FAITHFULNESS. AND YOU.

For over 75 years, we've witnessed God's faithfulness to the mission of Our Daily Bread Ministries. And we know that it's only with you, your families, your friends, your churches and your support that we've been able to share the good news of God's love, grace, and forgiveness all over the world.